UNHALLOWED
GRAVE

FRANK KARAN

Copyright © 2022 by Frank Karan.

ISBN- 979-8-8856-7248-1 (sc)
ISBN- 979-8-8856-7247-4 (hc)

All rights reserved. No part of this book may be reproduced or transmitted in any form or by any means, electronic or mechanical, including photocopying, recording, or by any information storage and retrieval system, without permission in writing from the copyright owner.

The views expressed in this work are solely those of the author and do not necessarily reflect the views of the publisher, and the publisher hereby disclaims any responsibility for them.

Matchstick Literary
1-888-306-8885
orders@matchliterary.com

ALIEN CLIQUE

I'm not punching straight upwards in the air
As a sign of expressively outward jubilation
I've been dealt a heavy handed crushing blow
I'm just venting, all my pent up frustration

That's pounced on me and restricted my bodily flow
It's ashamedly sad to see you hurt, an cryingly go
I feel like an astronaut; on some intergalactic trip
Adventurously mapping the farflung treacherous strip

Fascinatingly seeking out unseen and unchattered
Mysterious planets, I must be careful not to dip
It's as if I'm standing stark naked, in front of
A bedazzled non adoring audience of alien clique

ALWAYS THERE FOR ME

My love for you grows more and more each and
Every passing day; the thought of losing you
Makes me close up, cry then slowly wither away
To me you're like a heavenly angel in disguise

That's come to bless me, like a dormant sunrise
Especially when you twinkle your sparkling eyes
No matter what you may think or sadly say to me
You're always so lovely and always there for me

AMBIENT TOUCH

Your ambient touch is always etched
In me; it's even branded on my skin
It's warmer than the sun's rays
An quieter than the moon's gaze

Your crispy voice is somewhat silent
Tinging tenderly in my scooping ears
Serenading us each and every moment
Whilst calming all my pent up fears

You're enveloping arms totally enfold me
As supporting strength from angels wings
Protecting me wholly with a firm safely
Which only pure love can divinely bring

Which I can never honestly repay you
For the wonders you share in my life
I can more than ever be faithful
And forever be, your loving wife

ANTIQUE SCROLLS

Why don't you look underneath the iceberg for a change? As
You search to find the rainbow lining instead of the cloud
You're like a dying old tree trying to spurt fresh flowers
Memories of fragrances linger on but the freshness is gone

The children of the valley are playing with lost dolls
How can we decipher the dusty, tom up antique scrolls
is it up to us now to play the scared marvelous roles
We need to be careful not to disturb the ancient souls

AVOIDING THE AVALANCHE

It's like you've been wrapped up inside the icy mist
Of the ancient mountain, slopping down every crevice
And cradle, avoiding the avalanche reaching the fountain
The perspiration is profusely pouring out from your skin

The glimmer of hope, and some sense of salvation
Sparkles brightly from you're clinging inner eye
Metallic mirrors reflect the life that's gone by
Do you often think to have given it another try?

BATHLESS SORROW

After the absurdly ignominious display
From impolitically frugal disbursments
Involutely relishing in some satirical
Lyrical inpassionate symmetrical delay

We must remember to turn the sprinkles
On before there's a horrendous bushfire
Impassively we tend to chokingly refire
Asphixiating in heartthrobbing quagmire

Motherless children lye croaking thus soaking
In a bathless sorrow, out in the mean streets
They're future is staringly bleak; with ashen
Faces crying foul, then dispersing in retreat

Let's jump in my car, and drive over the dust covered roads
Heading strangely to a remotely
unknown country destination
Whre we can safely lose ourselves in a wonderless situation
Sharing our innermost desires in a gut wrenching application

BATTLE BRUISED BONES

I'm picking wildflowers by the bunch
As you finish off your Sunday brunch
Are you available for some x-mas lunch?
You can taste my exclusive mellow punch

You're moping around aimlessly, like a loafy
Tired shaggy sheepdog that's lost it's sheep
You better wake up now before you fall asleep
Your still throwing stones in the muddy creek

And hoping to resurface from this shallow sleep
When they do exhume you're battle bruised bones
It shall exhibit to the world what you've honed
Is love the gift, you wish you could have owned

BLACKDAMP

You're ponderability is slowly blustering
As you fragmented pale mind bristles out
Into various bizzare eclectic mangy forms
Eschewing the previous bereft wild storms

Neglectables can make delectable collectables
Walloping and burdening our discerning tastes
Do you expect a sudden case of high peripetia
Or the bludgeoning effects of ageing dementia

Gardantly, you silently sit and wonderously gape as the
Creeping blackdamp rapidly envelopes and suffocates you
Like a hyped up monstrous, homicidal adrenalized ape
Do you intend to visit, the almighty heaven's gate?

BLUNT REFUSAL

You're war wounds seldom flinch, as you're cross eyed
weary crying eyes peer up into the tall cobweb gables
All our stallions have been ransacked from our stables
My battlescard body has been depleted; but still able

There are lonely tears sulking out in the desert
If I run quick enough I can capture the pheasant
Thus outsmart the most corruptible devious peasant
It's such a cruel game but it can be very pleasant

Your righteous smile turns pale with the influxing gale
As you chew upon your own dry lips your burnt reddish
Face an sunken brittly eyes exhibit a contemptuous sour
Shricking afflication from a horridly inhospitable place

Your like an unhappy princess, desperately running into
The unknown, deepening dark, gloomy murky creepy forest
Just to escape the monotonous rigamarole and inefficient
Official protocol coupled with tedious worldly trappings

Anxiously you wait for prince charming to saddle up then
Mount his royal horse, and gallop right up to rescue you
Legions of adoring wellwishers wait,
for your inquisitive perusal
so why are you so undecided, and
still offer such a blunt refusal

BRAVING FUTILITY

A deadly silence greets us, at wattle daub cottages
Townspeople in gaudy, drabby robes pull their hoods
From over they're heads with dashingly mighty arms
Pointing silver daggers upwards with fearful armour

Peasants mumble with drying lips and sloshed tongues
Braving futility in dingy dark filthy strewn corners
Like lost sailors seeking the star in the unknown sea
This is a troubling worrisome place for anyone to be

Mutilated bodies lye dangling in the
stench deserted cobbled yard
Only an act of God could have saved us;
an not some knighted guard
Stools n' benches have been recklessly
overturned and badly broken
There's a mass of masonary dismembered
in our holy baptismal font

The old skinflint, wearing the magician's raggedy black cloak
Is not the sole perpetrator of this vile hideously sick crime
Scantly dressed maidens are hustled
up the quirky steps in front of
The chanting boys choir, quickly they
try to clean out the quagmire

BREATHLESS CHILL

There's the singing breathless chill
As the sunset spreads vibrant horizon
Colours, of slinky bright, gold and red
My lust for life has not been amply fed

I've learnt so much in these past cold dark nights
This halcyon of the light creepingly walks in disarray
Captured by the, misty fog clumsily wabbling from sight
As the twitching storms drive away the warming hot sun

And resplendent light, I yearn to hear a whisper of hope
Leaping strangely from the vapours of my clutching hands
Jumping in between the pillows and satin sheets of my bed
Can you hurry up and bring some love to my shivering head

BRISK WHISPER

You don't have to step aside just because your dream
Has died. I can feel you're pain sinking in my blood
But you haven't sunk in the torrid flood; intrusively
Boisterous is the vulgar philandering meandering thud

As the solar flares streak out of the blaring sun
The fire in your love ranches like volcanic charm
Firing a hail of bullets, filling me with dirty lead
and you're heart is aching for me to get back to bed

digging with blunt spades in the arid desert caves
there's a brisk whisper silently flushing the haze
but the still of the moment has no soul to pay
can you hear the many tongues whispering away?

CLOGGY MOAT

My body froze like it was floating in a
Cloggy moat; I was so badly bogged down
And miserably choking like a classic crying clown
Frantically I tried scrapping the excessive blood

From the problem stained Italian tiled marble floor
I went thru a bucket or two but u needed so much more
You're seemingly contradictory and oblivious when you
Deliberately speak of peace but you then plan for war

You seek to be certain to reach a devastating score
In reality you couldn't wipe the dust off the flor
What affluent mindless collusion, will you offer in
Exchange for a preeminent sophisticated conclusion?

COME AGAIN

There's a brand new thief in town
Stealing the hearts of poor souls
That are longing just to be found
Flitting vaccums of empty emotion

Whilst eloping into nocuous commotion
We can reach some comfort in our shed
Even in our stuffy worm out straw bed
Loftily I rest, my dreary shaggy head

Delicately succumbing to the feverish loving manic
Presiding zestfully over the amorous cupid's panic
I need a dose of you're love to penetrate me again
So I'm urging you to softly and swiftly come again

CONSTANTLY BATTERED

I have always trusted my heart before
And it's guided me to your front door
As I've travelled thru the meandering
Winding dusty roads driving past wild

Uninhabitable desert plains; a chill cements
Itself in my adrenalin changed boiling veins
The humid sunset sketches out dimmed shadows
Cactus plants shed they're aloe vera as they

Lay ripped n'torn, my heart feels like a cheap pawn
Our senses are constantly battered: deeply deformed
A menacing thought submitted in anger encircles with ease
You cannot begin to fathom, the vile coughing it's breeze

CONTROLLED PERMUTATION

Are you still chasing empty shallow illogical dreams
You've been snuggly wilted by other people's schemes
You're sensitivity n'creativity is bursting at the seems
Continually suffering from the dire loathing humiliation

There's an inner craving for a diplomatic correlation
Your like a bemusing, vulnerable pretty little flower
Perched on top of a delicately fragile wavering stalk
Left exposed to suffering from the provoking elements

Withering away from the burning sun and gusty windy rain
There's no adjusting remedy, only the impaired deviation
With the aching need for sought out controlled permutation
Let's dispense with the conflicting monotonous aggravation

CREEPINGLY JOLT

I was brought up with the black an white
Burnt out closed circuit t.v. in my head
Nowadays I creepingly jolt to the mirror
To confirm I'm alive; or dinically dead

It's days like these that I'd rather stay in bed
And browse over the books which I've dearly read
What's at the centre of your thick crummy bread
Do you still park your vintage rusty jag in the

Rat infested, spider webbed cobble stoned, leaking tiled shed
Elaborate silvery cups filled with frothing ale an heavy iron
Battle swords adorn your rowdy feast.
You've explored n' conquered
Many for off lands, paying homage to
their kings an rumbling cla

DEMENTED ID

You're desperately trying to crawl out of the rut
But you're hopelessly stuck in a hole; cul de sac
Vainly you attempt counselling out all of the muck
Though your still at loggerheads, with your pseudo

Intellectual demented id; that's why you frantically
Run around screaming, like an out of control mad kid
Secretly converting your angst on a high wire grid
Does a certain character trait set you up as bail?

Which trauma is associated with your psychoanalytical fate
Can you heal the searing wounds from this portentous state
That is culminating in a pitifully remorseful complexing rate
Wishfully you deserve a catharsis n' successively happier date

DEROGATIVELY FAINT

You won't need a heavy raincoat
If the rain has thritted away
You don't need a large ladder
If the chimney's just collapsed

But in my sombre arms you tenderly lapse
Your appearance is so demonstrably void
As you stealthily pounce like a lifeless android
Derogatively faith; and very superficially anoid

There must be a pirate ship full of treasure sinking in
You're mind, and you speedingly drive over the potholes
Filled with gunk, racing towards the
centuries old burnt out castle
Will you attempt to exorcise the ghostly
shadows without any hassle

DISTASTEFULL VICTORIES

I feel like I'm steadily walking on eggshells
When you're close to me as I keep hosing down
All the frustrations and tensions of the past
Thus I'm reconnecting to something worthwhile

That will gracefully and hopefully last
The notoriety associated with your name
It's only vainglorious at the very most
that's why I won't raise my cup to make

a cheerful toast. We shall not salute all the
distastefull victories that you proudly boast
perhaps you should head off to a warmer coast!
Maybe I'm reading cluelessly between the lines

But your parts appear like they've been
Stitched up at least half a dozen times
Do I think of something that can rhyme
If we stare at the sun, will it shine?

DISTILLED SHAME

You look so exclusively sexy and seductive
In your black pocker dot pink salmon dress
As you splash you're high class elongatedly
Fashioned style with cute tedisome laughter

You're farflung cautionary ideals are nothing
More than the dusty cobweb of a worrying mess
There are silly explanations for you're petty
Self afflicted, loathsome poppycock defeatist

Text; the innemonic movements speak highly n' praise
They subtly submerge swirling the murderistic test
Is there a need for cliché adoration or jubilation
When you project you're deadly archaic affiliation

What subliminal message can you denounce in your
Bogged down self doubting saturated souless brain
You're thought process has stunted, and is only to blame
Are there any benefits to reap from this distilled shame

DISTINCTIVELY FIDGETING

Fumbling thru the pages of you're
Disenchanted moderate frowzy life
Distinctively fidgeting, on a cul de sac
In the messy warehouse of academic quack

You're like a pitilessly frozen flower
Immersed within a frosty winter's tale
Unlending to a strange bewitching fairytale
Our emotional state, does episodically fail!

Leaving a dislodged juxtaposition trail
Then we grow stylishly sordid and frail
Disinvolving ourselves in a murky sinking
Fruitless cocktail! So where do we avail?

DUBIOUS ATTRITION

You're not a gentleman scholar; plainly your
Always reading journals of scientific fodder
Can you detect any difference living in your
Immaculate, counter culture proof safe haven

We're still sending legions of persistent colonists
To dominate the notoriously untamed distant regions
There's some dubious attrition circulating multiple
Derogatory transitions within you're disturbed mind

I really don't love you, like a long lost brother
But we keep running blindly n'openly to eachother
Even if we're kayaking wildly into the downstream
With such ferocious austerity that is seldom seen

I'm trying to clean, the mercilessly heavy cannon
As I'm unwittingly winning the game of backgammon
I'm trying to sell you the benefits n' not the bones
Before we all become, the next generation of clones

ENUNCIATE

Is there some fanciful rainbow in your dream
What sweet favourable obsession do you sceam
Are you trying to tell the water to run upstream
Do you familiarize yourself with the common team

Will you still wonder where is the frothy cream
So why do you look at a situation as a problem?
And roll around in the mud like a gruntling pig
Do you still wish to fly even if you lack wings

Why must you propitiate yourself with an awful mean ache
Maybe you need to clean things out with a farmer's rake?
How nimble is your erroneously miscalculated sad mistake
Do you meticulously enunciate whatever else is at stake?

EXHAUSTING SUN

Adorning the galactic nightsky with a blazing red
Candle on my wilted fingertips in front of my eye
The exhausting sun is drying out our precious planet
As weathered stones burn our pressable walking shoes

The copper skies n'ochre cliffs fall victim
To the insatiable, fire hungry ravaged bush
As the dying earth hastily devours torrents
Of rain; which combine to soothing the pain

Walk softly on the worn out timber floor
And try to leave behind the hurt that
You felt before; we'll keep out the cold
And I'll comfort you till we grow old

EXPLICIT INNUENDO

You're sapio sexual greed, outlasted every need
Concatenating in a variety of explicit innuendo
Swapping fact for fiction, by elocution diction
Serving past intellectual stimulating addiction

I will gloriously show you angelic white haven
After you've shown me the bleakest darkest hell
Perhaps we'll be seduced by it's poignant spell
As we hurriedly race to ring the embattled bell

You're so prudishly dull that your pathetic mind
Must be capped; distastefully annulled and zapped
Are you still chasing foxes which eate the hens?
Or vainly searching for diamonds among the pens?

FIERCE INDICTMENT

I'm drifting between the mellow in picturesque channels
Displaying unfaltering control n' superb manipulation
What consensus can we reach for our turbulent nation
Do we have the will to stay away from all temptation

May it be dearly enough to bring us appropriate salvation
Or will we continue to suffer the humiliating degradation
There's fierce indictment so ever whimsically portrayed
It's like rolling onto the slippery snow; without a slade

FLASHING WARNINGS

You're gentle words patiently vibrate thru my soul
Awakening an racing like thoughts in the fast lane
The flames in my heart have now been patiently lit
There's ambient flashing warnings of costs n' writs
I've thoroughly exhausted all my possibilities
Are there any alterior motives or disabilities
I'm shaking n' guivering as I voice all my fear
Quickly I try to grab you before you disappear

Amongst the darkening shadows I frantically search
So I can revive myself an not be left in the lunch
I'm so anxiously delighted n' excited that I'm yours
An that you can hug me with your tender loving paws

FLINCHING WOUNDS

You hide you're shame, so hypnotically well
As the flotilla of pain navigates your cell
There's sudden burst of rigorous energy
Delivered from your stonefaced encallowed

Shell. The ground still shakes as you tred so
Hurriedly and abruptly like a ferocious swell
Do you expect a prestigious emdument from the
Fond memories of our dearly beloved deceased

In my grandmother's old closet chest, the silver
Coloured vests; wither amongst fragrantly exotic
Flumes; marching in tempo with melodious tunes
Engrossing the enchashment of flinching wounds

FOREVER STAY

You make me smile like no one else can
I treasure the time that I hold your hand
I wish to give everything to you my dear
With you by my side I have nothing to fear

Youre all think about every night n'day
I miss you so much, when you're far away
In my arms I hope that you forever stay
So come along and play with me today!

GASPING LAYERS

Slothily you curiously ask me for sound advice
But you only have to ask me one and not twice
Your transitory pose reflects how you presuppose
Then you shreek like a priest at the royal feast

You're face is riddled with guilt as you bite your upper lip
A loathing hateful guilt brews stealthily in your coffee cup
Sacredly quit you shabbily hurry amongst darkening shadows
Odiously mumbling your sacred prayers
as you so comfortably

Sit, flagging yourself on top of the colossal Everest seat
There's a circle of destruction, impassively at you're feet
Drifting past the pent up gasping layers of fermenting trouble
Trying to avoid the heavy rumblings
of the fast moving shuttle

HEAVILY OSTRACISED

You seem to be irrespressibly lame, as you're
Heavily ostracise in this marginalized game
This gutsy willy saga, is not your classic thriller
It's so mysteriously compelling; as a spine chiller

There's a languid assorted beauty navigating amongst
Theatrical dynamics and specific dreamlike mechanincs
Out characters are suitably played, whilst the stage
Props are meticulously sorted and cleverly displayed

There are no unwilling participants in this play
Antagonistically stigmatized between the creative
Expression of a strikingly simple yet affable plan

Accelerating technological innovation, with fantasized
Stimulation; celebrating a sensationalistic transition
Cordially we mic up our cocktails and hope to live happily
Ever after, but our barcode pass is denied the there after

HIDDEN TREASURES

You're just let the genie out of the magic bottle
Which has been locked away for thousands of years
Now it's time to taste her angst and lonely tears
Do we decipher the dialogue of hieroglyphic fears
We've been neglecting these vast hidden treasures

Which have been secretly tucked away
in a myriad of dungeons
Thru evolving generations causing needles chaotic sensations
What can we consume n' contribute
from history's elusive past
There's an illusion of winning awkward, rolling in the flask
Whittling very fast! Is there a renaissance which will last?

HORRID LITTLE DREAM

Your like a trooper in an old grey beat up jeep
Driving over rattling stones jolting my bones
I feel like a tortoise cooking in a dense shell
Soaking in a boiling pot, bubbling steaming hot

As you glaringly smile n'lick your red glossy lips
I'll gently kiss you down to your silky fingertips
Your saddening face reflects it's Mona Lisa Smile
Hastily jerking to escape the dirty measly chores

You secretly crave to be whisked away to the great outdoors
Unwittingly stumbling onto lost civilizations ancient doors
You're hotly contested alimony is nudged within sour cream
Do you hear the primal scream? In your horrid little dream

HUFFINGLY PUFF

Your mind is bubbling like cheap flaky window film
Sputtering simplistic cunning lies, just to get by
Are you still watering the drought tolerant plants
You look like you can build a church without pants

So please don't get a heart attack along the way
While mixing the exotic pebbles with cement clay
Why do you still stand on the wrong side of the fence
Then continue to poke fun at those you consider dense

Running like a bee stung bull around the sports arena
You huffingly puff so bloodied and dangerously meaner
I miss the open air spaciousness and eccentric graciousness
Ascribing to an assertively adorned; towering tenaciousness

ICEBERG TIP

I frantically grabbed your hands with a
Python's grip an dragged you out of the
Suzzy rockpool, as we interlocked but still
Managed to miss eachother's honeycombed lips

The angry volcano spewed it's molten lava
Way above our gullible faint little heads
Hastily we raced down the showy mountain sled
Then me tried to find shelter in our cosy bed

What escape is there from mother nature's trip?
And the dark jungle eludes is dangerously quick
We must seek an exit plan so we can safely slip
Thus avoid; the ominously powerful, iceberg tip

IMPREGNABLE COCOON

You've locked yourself in a totally isolated vicinity
Without any movable agility awkwardly reeling ashamed
Indefensibly cowering in a state of delayed shock as you
Carefully conceal the hidden scars, and invisible wounds

In your impregnable cocoon; yet you
become downtrodden like a
Bafoon! Can you still afford to eat with a shiny silver spoon
The shackles of anonymity will hopefully
be unchained real soon
And you shall be released from this
barbarous torturous platoon

IMPRESSIVE DISPLAY

You're panting and sweating profusely, like a
Thoroughbred racehorse that's just ran over a
Mile in less than a couple of quick minutes
There's an asphyxiating tone in your breath

When you hesitantly jump out of the aeroplane
Without a parachute to your own sudden death
Do you wonder who will catch you before you fall
It's a dazzling synthesis for impressive display

As I lay witness to the weirdness at my dismay
Submerging myself with ethereal fear and doubt
My tired body begins to drooly sway in the droopy
Couch! Will we avoid the turmoil without a stouch

INEVITABLE DISASTER

I've suffered a horrible death by a thousand cuts
The arsenic keeps whiplashing thru my tender guts
I'm so undeniably keen to get to the fixating crux
An find a solemn moment to mediate inside our huts

But time is renowned as a mercilessly cruel master
Unfortunately we cannot turn back the paring clock
Or slow down it's weighty chop as we age much faster
How can we carefully avoid, the inevitable disaster?

INNUMERABLY FINE

Playfully you wrap you're warm chubby legs
Around mine, careening out the wintry cold
It's a very pleasant feeling, sensually entwined
Our loving moves are so sweetly innumerably fine

Grundgingly I'm fired up as you embossom me
Triumphantly letting me know that your mine
You're like a fearsome mighty apache warrior
Proudly parading in the colossal Grand Canyon

Openly firing our Winchester rifle into
The vast unfriendly, lonely desert place
You're bullets keep on ricocheting off the
Dusty mountain rocks, far into empty space

Regurgitating in a furiously wild inhospitable place
You roam around endlessly without any fear or disgrace
Petulantly trying to rekindle you're former glory in some post
Authentic native space! Do you believe
you can save you're race?

INTANGIBLE LIBIDO

You remind me of an amateur boxer that's trying
To jab and punch above his bodyweight; randomly
Weaving n' ducking as you throw the punches at
Your opponents body, needlessly it's too late

You'd prefer to sheepishly lye on the couch
Than to get yourself tangled up in a stouch
Why don't you watch an old time silent movie
Then dance the night away and feel so groovy

Excuse the noisy racket while I switch my heavy navy jacket
Is you're phobia registering in the mode of placid placebo?
Or are you retracting from an invaluable intangible libido?
All of your confronting thoughts have bottomed out to zero!

INTERACTIVE COIL

You're like a slimy sea urchin ventilating in
The moist soil, feeding on a decaying platter
Pretending to be a scientific genius; developing
New theories n' discovering strange cosmic matter

You may place the gun straight onto you're head
But the chamber lacks the revolving bullet lead
You're life is like a river carving out valleys
N'carrying away debris of rock, the crying wind

Lies filled with grains of twisting sand
Sculpturing with grains of twisting sand
Sculpturing various climatic desert land
Perhaps we can drill deep enough to find
A new reservoir of sustainable crude oil

There has to be some useful interactive coil
To inveigle the supply in undiminishing foil
We'll be inundated with more than gas an oil
Making invaluable the price of your hard toil

INWARDLY STUTTERING

You're like a general without a trained army
Giving orders with authority but no military
You're insincere smile, grovels like a little child
Inwardly sluttering with a naïve drooping muttering

You're aim is tense an practically dense
You've lost the innings but won the game
The prize of winning is always the fame
You've hit the ball but it bounces back

You get so mad, that you blow your slack
Revenge is swift n' reassuringly on track
You'd had to break out of the prison cage
Now you've been exalted n' can lazily rage

IRREDUCIBLE STAMINA

Enviously I'm drooling at your irreducible stamina
It's so intractably refractive, notching up points
There must be a resume listing all the lazy joints
For you're intra mundane, socially active calendar

Are you stubbornly selective or a sincere skeptic
Are you a scientific realist or a hippie idealist
Why make a giant problem out of little nothing
I'm so fed up with the regular petty muttering

Is there a framework of functionality needling amidst
The disgusting loathing turmoil which you boil n'bake
I'm seemingly fluctuating in a lofty lonesome space
Will I be released tenderly, without a cosmic trace

I'VE MADE MISTAKES

I've wasted time, but you know I don't really mind
I've made mistakes, but we all have our lad breaks
I still keep on trying each n'every day, even if
It's hard for me to make it, this ole flimsy way

I wish to have it all, so I'm constantly treading
Carefully not to fall into the wrong rowdy stall
We can lodly laugh and rage at the local amusement
Hall, and end up playing in the Grand Concert Hall

JAGGEDLY DANCE

As I suddenly race towards you
In the hot steamy tropical sun
There's no sensible system of logic
Which pervades us to having any fun

The crescent flame is highly insoluble
And mildly deferable to more than some
Our custom designed jungle flannelette suits
Rhythmically march like khaki military boots

It's a certain style that we handsomely wear
Even if we don't have spaced out frizzy hair
We can make the paparazzi shrivel n' rifling
When we jaggedly dance all night and sing

JAUNTILY DESULTORY

You're locked in a prison of loneliness
Desecrating any caring feministic touch
Whilst departing with abstract cheery motion
You degust at an honourary solitary devotion

Possessing slightly limited knowledge
Supplanting into holy ancient storage
Your life style is jauntily desultory
Vaguely concealing ice cold purgatory

Which courtship or lordship, should you serve?
The art of pleasing a soulful mate is at stern
Your like a wet piece of wood that needs to be
Kiln dried. Don't you know how hard I've tried

KINETIC FRENZY

The kinetic frenzy of hatred is gaining unwavering
Unprecedented momentum leaving us frozen with fear
There's a throttling of the tongue, as in innocent
Young man lies badly bleeding till he's justly won

This event is frighteningly real, as I
implicitly consider all aspects
Of a burdening touching feel; dissecting
the corpse is such a big deal
Shall I now londge my pretty appeal? It's
akin to changing deckchairs on
A sinking ship! Is it wiser to invest upon
a waterspout tropical trip?

LAST PICTURE

That was the last picture which I had of you
It looked so faint but bluntly true, the hot
Emotion I can't refrain, for it pivotes like
A furious burning flame, standing light on a

Stall so proud and robustly tall. How bright
Do you gleam? Like some sparkling laser beam
Working your glorious sweet way is wonderfully
Cute leaving me mute, that's all I have to say

LED ASTRAYED

The werewolf howls up at the dronish moon
It's hungry eyes n'bloodied paws makes it
Devilishy reflective. I'm so spellbound an held
Quite irrationally than unintentionally captive

Running thru the mildewy darkening forest
To escape the onsetting calamitous plague
Hastily I trip over the quicksand sprayed
I'm not at all bemused or terribly afraid

I think I might have weepily overstayed
I'm that tired and desperately depraved
I've treaded cautiously n'battled brave
Rescuing souls, which were led astrayed

LOOTING YOURE VIRGIN SOUL

The shadow of the serpent, hungrily spreads it's
Claws all over you, casting it's reign of terror
You cower beneath a blood soaked, moth infested old
Dirty wollen blanket, trying to shake off the cold

Which demons are still looting your virgin soul
Plaguing and ravaging you, till your inner bone
The hatred you've experienced, exudes the vicious
Flesh tearing an mind boggling shattering torment

Desperately you prey to find a cure but your not pure
The scientific analysis; often leads you to paralysis
Can we exorcize the diabolical hideous creatures with
All their monstrosly wicked, hate infesting features

MACHIAVELLIAN CURSE

You look so very shaken, battered and pale
Your hands keep trembling on the guardrail
Did the love of your life drastically fail
But your not that old and handsomely frail

It must have left you whailing like a whale
As you keep aiming for the elusive bullseye
Yet you only manage to score the outer rail
You toss you're love away, like a worthless

Disregarded throw away, chocolate wrapper
Then you wonder what on earth is a matter
You always wish to fatten up your soiled empty purse
But you're a descendant from the achiavellian curse

MENTAL ANNEXATION

You're ego is like a gushing wound which will never heal
There's a centripetal force, distilling original content
Sudden subtle reminders are the hagiographies of the past
Whilst momentarily forgetting, then indignantly rejecting

Populistic measures locked in futuristic cybernetic treasures
Inordinately teasing the highly contestable trialing measures
Unfulfilled promises cause mental
annexation, which may occur
Compositionally sustained and altered into the key of discord

Seedling austerity is enthusiastically agreed n'proportionately
Decreed, your tormented life reveals
the widening cracks in the
Ceiling! Developing the less envied
repertoire of broken dreams
Tipping over on unsavoury Ilk;
incubating in your mother's milk

MIND BOGGLING CATHARSIS

You're like a kid in the appetizing lolly shop
Filing up the bay with a glucose licorice choc
Delicately riding the wave of ecstasy till you drop
Unsatedly famished with a chink and a wavering flop

Hoodwinking your ego into a mind boggling catharsis
The household fixtures n'fittings are semi detached
Shall we attempt to salvage any portable collectible antique
Or will the existentialist creed deliver us a superior bread

MUCH MALIGNED

Your like a parasitic withering tree that's trying to
Spurt fragrant flowers as you seek to find the silver
Lining instead of the crystallizing dark rainy clouds
They're are many wicked tongues, percolating the much

Maligned, outlandishly crawling up the wall like ants
Why don't you look underneath the chilly icebergs for
A change? Instead of staring confusedly at flavoured
Icecaps in your forbidden mind; assuredly you easily

Walk in the dreamscapes of soothingly hot bubbly mud
Replenishing your spirit confluently in misty rivers
Before I lugubriously slip into the tropical sandy sea
Thus avoiding the torrid hailstorm of torment and plea

MYSTICAL SERENADE

You've been very disrespectably apprenhensive, when
You denounced and striped me mercilessly, I was so
Unimpendingly tired, as you're tailwind swept through
Like ruins of a siege, you deliberately caught me off

Guard, as I was preparing myself for apocalyptic battle
Staunchingly you were ergotly chasing, many wild cattle
Abating from some lost love dimension; in cupid's storm
Abruptly streaking down the narrow laneway was the norm

Appeasing the gods, in a hellish mystical serenade form
Serving refreshing dark wine and tropical fruit on time
Reproachfully scrounging then drinking cool fruity lime
Were all you're adventurous escapades as humble as mine?

NERVE RACKING

You're sailing frantically against the oceanic tide
But you cannot escape the furious ghostly shipwreck
You wish to be lucky and jump over the flaming fire
Without collecting a smouldering burn upon the tyre

Occasionally you will cordially dance intensely higher
It's annoyingly humiliating and explicitly frustrating
Manifesting the encoded fountainhead of your archenemy
Into a severed aligning nerve racking descending twine

What pseudo intellectual connotations shall you employ
To enable the natural adventurous sexual exploitations
I suppose you'd like me to pour honey into your frothy
Steamy bubbles, then drink the soapwater from the bath

NICE TO MEET YOU

I would wish to wake up early everyday
To the sound of your breath on my neck
The warmth of your red lips kissing my check
The touch of your fingers sliding on my skin

An the sound of your heart beating with mine
Makes me heartlovingly and pleasantly unwind
I once was scared to start all over again, but
For now, it's nice to meet you, my dear friend

NUMBING STENCH

There's a darkness enslaving, my volatile heart
It's wicked claws pierce right thru like a dart
Your love is like a window to the shining sun
It happily opens up with so much excitable fun

I feel like I'm dancing on mountainous thin air
Because my feet levitate, without a single care
Do i still awkwardly stand an wonderously stare
At the burning rainforests without anyone there

There's a burst of crude anger crying silently
As you stubbornly sit upon the impartial bench
Waiting for a verdict to ease the numbing stench
Where will you fall? When you slip off the fence

OBSESSIVE STRUGGLE

Can you recall any relevant harrowing tales
From you're impoverished relatives? Sifting
Thru the garbage bags with hunger screeching
Out of their eyes n'empty stomachs trying to

Get by: the repulsive stench of human rights
Abuses, is not what anyone literally chooses
Embracing an era for humanity, with a fragile
Piece of sanity! Do pardon my inane profanity

It may be forgotten or downtrodden but not that dead
This tormenting obsessive struggle buried in my head
Reclusively denying my right for a flight to fantasy
It's just not so easy, simply striving to stay ahead

OFTEN REARRANGED

You're schmaltzy imported elegant chandeliers
Cast a whirling chiaroscuro onto the ceilings
Providing the imperilling crystal capped filter
Rancorously illuminating warm intimate feelings

The antique mahogany chairs are emblematically designed
Offering a non intrusive, yet comfortably relaxing nook
Enjoyably warming n'drying your wet clothes by the fireplace
The aristocratic marble floor an decorative plinths worthily

Complement the stained glass hay windows and rugged oak
Sliding doors, coupled with chesterfield styled lounges
Which is often rearranged, to satisfy you're eccentric
Art noveau specific taste? So why are you been chased?

OPEN JAWS

There are motherless children crying in the wind
They're sad sorrow echoes emptiness into my skin
Yet you look so tremendously appealing with you're
Button holed shirt opened way down onto your waist

It oozes so much sexyness an vigorously exuberant taste
With limitless resources of resplendedness repelling me
From the distinguishable miserly mistake; hurriedly you
Try to snatch a disaster, from the open jaws of failure

But now it's accessibly gone, from too little too late
There is no sweepstakes racing carnival at your parade
Only a rotating wrecking ball which veraciously rolls you
Further down, into the sharp bitterness of life's charade

PERCUSSIVE BRAINCHILD

Strange creatures inhabit the darkest corner's of
You're stalking rambling innermost fathomless mind
Are you reluctant to expose they're wincing brooding
Features, and drink their intoxicatingly putrid wine

Bulking up is you're naive ego. It's reintroducing the
Pent up desires akin to driving on a wornout flat tyre
Inadvertently colliding in a big feisty non sequential
Perennial thought process, then left quite shamelessly

Pandering the troubling mess we're still charmingly naughty
Yet cagerly receptive, to get our lives back in perspective
You look like your shirt is torn an dangling off the scruff
of your neck, maybe that's why your always so out of breath

Your juxtapositional life reads like a comic script
And you openly admit that you've had a bizzare rift
Is that the simultaneous prodigy with a funny story
So what is the percussive brainchild, of your glory

PITHILY LAME

I met a girl but didn't even get her name
She ignited my heart, like a hungry flame
We danced all night n'she put me to shame
We went to bed yet she wasn't at all tame

I rose up in the morning after our lover's game
I felt so ticklish but it wasn't the sweet same
All the other loves just seemed so pithily lame
She's descendant from a planet laviously insane

PITINGLY SORROWFUL

As the greyish night clouds disperse
An the waxing moon encroaches on our
Pitingly sorrowful starry eyed cameo faces
Gleaming in souless wintery shallow traces

I'm frantically elbowing my way through
The thick forest brandies whizzing over
Muddied leaves and camouflaged quicksand
Past abandoned burnt out haunted ranches

Ghostly is the feel of this unpleasant night
Ghastly is the zeal of this ghoulish delight
Nymphs keep singing whirring songs, unmelodiously
Transported by the diabolical howling chilly wind

There are mermaids in the sea struggling to be
Free, there's no sympathy or comfort to be had
Or even a happy smiling face, which is not sad
Did I experience a devilish nightmare too bad

PRISM RAINBOW

We have to cease having shallow fun
Because the nightmare has just begun
There's not enough water to fill the lake
Or unsalted butter to bake the cheesecake

You appear so flamboyant with your turtle neck
Sweater pressing up against your grovelly neck
What I seek to calmly do is to delve into your
Bittersweet silent loneliness then subtly peck

I'd gladly fly to the shining craterous moon
If I knew when I could happily have you back
Will you be able to build me a prism rainbow
Before I blast off and blow my flaming stack

PROSECUTORS ARMS

Running around like some excited action packed
Comic book superhero, nullifying the ingenious
Villainous escapades to nothing more than zero
Your exploits uncanningly deliver as from evil

Dominantly amending the warchest and downtrodden
Hero's vest, you can not afford to cry over sour
Grapes, concealing the armoury of crusading capes
As your deeds grow notorious and your name reigns

Glorious! The criminals are becoming
hauty an ever increasingly
Despicably naughty, entering the city
like scurrilous vagabonds
With nothing else on they're sinister
conniving evil minds than
Wreaking havoc by plotting annoyingly
upstaged grandiose crimes

Diligently you arrest an escort them into the awaiting
Prosecutor's arms, stealthily an meticulously dethrone
Them of they're enticingly smirky, hideous vice charms
What more can be done? Before we sound the loud alarms

PSYCHOTIC THRILL

We're still indulging in eminent abstract rhetoric
As my sweaty senses move towards seemingly blurred
I try to quickly salvage all that I possibly can
So the important things will not get out of hand

I know that it's time for me to make a positive stand
Do you honestly think you can swallow the poison pill
And dimax to a euphoric everlasting psychotic thrill
The mere thought of it leaves me with a shivery chill

It's so dangerously exciting an uninhibitingly inviting
Fiery dragons prowl grim dungeons, tenaciously fighting
The adrenalin rush oversees the menacing pulsating lust
This psychotic thrill is demonstrably very overpowering

RAMPANT IDEALISM

Is there some rampant idealism or a bit
More devious sinister schism? Uprooting
Your dogmatic preconceived, permanently
Ingrained values; condemning your pride

Causing you to landslide aimlessly down the tall
Icecaped mountains and pristine Snowclad valleys
Tumbling over geysers n'hot water bubbly springs
The floodtides unrepentantly combine the vintage

Rare source of appreciatively embraced, mutually
Corresponding so workably and indefinably serene
Why do we always run into a pattern of irregularities?
Bursting at the seems! Can we counteract these schemes

RESIDUAL RUMINATION

We have to perceive a spuming, residual rumination
Especially after the long bumpy wild ruckling ride
That curtails us to rise up with a positive stride
Are we sick of letting life just aridly us by

Is individual freedom a privilege or a choice
Can we speak loudly without a sickening voice
Are we still totally manipulated and suppressed
Do we have the courage to see what is the best?

How many balls are they're left bouncing high in the air
Do we honestly care? Can we plug every gap or take a nap
Is there any demarcation process of internal division
Augmenting some soap opera agenda without supervision

REST MY WEARY SOUL

You don't have to wear expenssive business suits
Or chase after far fetched ideological pursuits
Come with me and I'll take you to a place where
The sun never sets; and the stormy clouds shine

My heart feels like it's floating outwards in space
When all I'm really seeking is a safe resting place
Can you stop fidgeting by looking so unashamedly rude
I'm drooling at your curves as I draw you in the nude

I've given up, trying to surf the colourful rainbow
Or even finding the fabled leprechaun's pot of gold
There's no endearing legacy to set unattainable goals
I'd rather grow comfortably old an rest my weary soul

RIGID REFUSAL

There's a negatively charged rigid refusal
Emanating from your blustery crooked stare
You're relentless snoring trait, is caping
A mundane dizzily confusing middling stale

The love that we had often measured, so
Unassumingly well lies gutterly swollen
Into broken fragments, especially after
You've been left shanghaied, there's no

Place for you to hide, you can only hope to
Surt the swelling tide as you don't have so
Much time to bide, then you wish to sail the
Stream with pride and have love by your side

SO SAD INSIDE

She creepingly walks to the window
Peeping out from the curtain blind
Into the rain; into the pain
Into someone else's shame

There's something that she needs to
Know, but doesn't openly show
She's so sad inside
Her tears are thwart with pride

She's so sad inside
Maybe she can safely run n'hide
In another town an place
You can change your face

You shall hide your race
You don't have to give your name
To play the lover's game
Just pull the trigger n'aim

She's so sad inside
Her tears are thwart with pride
She's so sad inside
Maybe she can safely run n'hide

SOILED BROOM

My patience Is so rapidly wearing thin
As the tension is brimming off my skin
I'm levitating over the greyish clouds
Into the uplifting sedate bluish skies

Straight above you're watchful eye
It feels like all the air has been
Sucked out of this seedy room
Flying upwards in a helium balloon

Now I'm sweeping above left over ashes
With an old raggedy straw soiled broom
Spring is here and I'm waiting for the
Flowers to bloom n'take away the gloom

SPONGY COMPROMISE

You hover high in the air like a hungry
Eagle whose getting ready to swoop down
On some lazily swimming unsuspecting fish
There are many angry faces lurking behind

The cliche facade of expensive leafy suburbs
Left so emotionally destitute, and hungry to
Strike at the outlandish extravagance promised
To them whish is nothing more than a pipedream

With fear and hurt best in they're faith searching
Drooping eyes. aren't we fed up with all their lies
There must be some change to bring about a surprise
Why should we settle for a meagre spongy compromise

STREAMLINED IN EDICT

Your beeping behind the sluggish nobility
Whilst dreading the hypocritic mediocrity
You're wonderfully sophisticated and self assured
You shun the limelight yet your so bitterly bored

Streamlined in edict so compact and delicate
Amazingly bewildering is the love you behold
You're diligently smooth n'surprisingly bold
Proudly we recycle all that is deemed as old

The turn it into pretty wealthy glorius gold
There are many swooning sweet songs to be sung
In your honour; with much overdue praise, we can
Set the entire town ablaze, in a stupendous haze

SULRY SWEET CARES

Her tears drip down the drapery
I can see that she's really not
All that she wants to be; my heart
Feels hard the pain, that sustains

But I'm not to blame, even if our love
Is so much the same; full of rasp vain
I'd like to catch her on my fast plane
So we both can train, intensely insane

Underneath her sultry, sweet caress
I'm breveting full of lustfull zest
Stinging fast like a squirming pest
Whose vieing to rest on her warm breas

TALLISH MIRRORS

Your as sneaky as a slimy sewer rat
Wheezling down the filthy drainpipe
You're unblemished demeanour yearns
To escape from it's problematic past
Unbiddening are some tallish mirrors

Reflecting the torment that you hide
The years keep reeling when we slide
Beckoning towards the trinkets of our
Narrowly missed love, we are like the
Captives concealed in a leather glove

TANTALISINGLY BRISK

Don't you think it's time? To shrugg off
Your nervously timid tedious inhibitions
By fulfilling all your awkward ambitions
I'm sick of the eversible rapacious lies

Covertly elucidating soft rampart charm
Huggingly beneath your warm bulging arm
Manic love sulks so tantalisingly brisk
Dwindling the propagating meddling risk

If you won't accept my doleful existence
You'll be besieged, with firm resistance
Nevertheless I do admire your rampant persistence
It's because of that, I will pledge my assistance

TENDER WOMB

There's a special world for you n'me
A magical bond where many cannot see
It wraps us up in it's shallow cocoon
Gripping fiercely in it's tender womb

It's fingers spread like fine spun gold
Gently wrestling us to the blessed fold
Like oolen thread, it holds us fast
Memories like these are meant to last

Though at times; a thread may break
A new one forms softly in it's wake
To bind us close and keep us strong
In a special world, where we belong

THUNDERCLOUD ECLIPSE

The sweetness has evaporated from your lips
As your life has been tossed away like some
Cheap useless thumbnailed office paperclips
The loneliness descends deeper into another

Long drawn out saga, hastily you drown away your
Sorrows by drinking ale and cans of bitter lager
The steamy sunshine horizontally dips into a
Mesmerizingly turbulent thundercloud eclipse

Fond memories often cvade us, and we always need
to participate in a variety of comforting tricks
There is a desperate struggle in my heart, as it ticks
The petiness of love an laughter preside, so it clicks

TORMENTING PAST

The rsetless ghosts of the tormenting past
Have envenomated your fiendish bodily soul
Blasting you're ego as you fall from grace
It's such a sad n'lonely imperilling place

Like a tough guienlessential prize fighter
Fatally knocked n'collapsing to the ground
Hitting the rugged smelly canvass facedown
Then rebounding to collect his royal crown

Trading insults n'vulgar obscenities, whilst
Deliberating mildly with solitude n'serenity
To the approving accolades from adoring fans
Maybe we can invigorate, some positive clans

TREMENDOUS THUNDER

You're the girl with the long, blond bleached hair
The raggedy smile, prospect face n'worldly grace
That I felt in love with so many happy years ago
You've admirably perfected my stop start then go

Your like a witty naughty colourful, little clown
Throwing insinuations, and temptations hands down
But I am no longer blind so I cannot really see
What treachery do you still hide from honest me

There's a tremendous thunder rampaging thru my soul
The splendour of your charm enlightens me even upon
My unhappiest days, I swirve over the darkening haze
You're luxurious lips bring an unannounced happiness

As we now attempt to look so much healthier n'slender
The ecosystem in your mind has cascaded into oblivion
There's no stellar consulation from a far fetched constellation
Are all of your artificial, arterial routes back in circulation

UNEASY LONELINESS

Have you ever seen the cloudy sun set
In you're dusty foggy rearview mirror
It's not only reddish orange n'yellow
But a preview to a reascending mellow

Can you always see the end of a tunnel
When it's the reverse of a dark funnel
Why ask a question when the question is
The answer. What again is the question?

I smelt the sweat off your olive skinned hairy back, as i
Scrolled my faintly painted finger nails down your spine
I sensed an uneasy loneliness; humble but not yet divine
Embracing the irregular beat of your heart, like a chime

UNEXPLAINED TEARS

Children's fantasies become lost
With puzzling unexplained tears
The winter's grow much longer
Over the ageing lonely years

When summer arrives we will
Rejoice with a healthy hand
But the trick; is to absorb
Whatever is at your command

You're like a one legged bird! That's
Trying to find a place to safely land
I'm so happily singing, songs of love
Whilst merrily dreaming and sheeming

I'm thoughtfully an shrewdly deeming
And thinking of nostalgic foreseeing
I'm still struggling to siphon out those
Sad unexplained tears which are steaming

UNHALLOWED GRAVE

Are we going to conquer some strange new land
Or sink smoothly in the soft marshy quicksand
I'm no better than you or I: I just stimulate
Whatever I like to try even if I'm rather shy

You're so blaze when you cordially say
That butter doesn't melt in your mouth
You're imagining that you're waltzing
On top of snowcapped hollow mountains

But in reality you're falling from
Double storey townhouse apartments
And waffering onto the dirty sidewalk
Pacing down the ochre smelly laneways

Bumping into the vices of vicious hard core punks!
That are drinking out of empty bottles like skunks
Why do we have to suppress the antidote for drunks
Who have we conquered an who will be luckily saved

Is there a finale to this loathsome game?
Indecently wrestling ourselves with shame
What else shall we humanitarianly crave
Resting in the shallow unhallowed grave

UNMITIGABLY FLAWED

You're undying gratitude an persuasive affection
Culminates in a desired kaleidoscope of detection
There's a huge difference from swimming leisurely
In the ocean to jumping over bulging river stories

Maybe you miss something that you've never had
Is this why you always appear so miserably sad
There's more to life than been melancholic glad
You easily revel high in vainglorious sensation

Which must urgently deliver a sense of exhiltation
Desperately you move up the ladder but your clawed
And sunken posture is submerging unmitigably flawed
You look so faintly out of it. Are you still bored?

UNPRECEDENTED AMENDMENT

You're outlandishly wild exploits, have been documented
The bizzare extracts aren't simply just one dimensional
Pincushioning the excessive distaste of your monotonous
Mundane tone. Will you ever stop from dialing the phone

Is there a pseudonym or fancy pursenicketing favourite
Are you still trying to unearth some ancient important
Archaeological sites or just lazily meander through
Various unsalvaged disenfranchised, neolithic rites

Your roving fascination, delves deeply into antiquity
But you seem like your still paying above award rates
Just to go an watch the same old ratbag boring circus
Yet you're neoclassical designs spectacularly feature

Many finely crafted intricately woven exotic lines
Is there a grizzly find amongst the nursery rhymes
There must be a logical comparitive compendium, in order to
Dignify the diversely painstacking,
unprecedented amendment

UNUSUAL UNDERSTANDING

There's no sudden flurry of support
As you strike the magic zero naught
Questions are not always openly asked
Yet remain after the event has passed

Transactions are not meant to be visible
But we bargain with our hearts divisible
There are no series of recommendations luridly
Abbreviated in hard to follow pencil citations

Is there some pronounced significance to you're
Exemplary catchery exhuming the fragile standby
Shall we masticate in mutual unusual understanding
Terribly depicting the eccentric uncertain pending

VAGRANT DISEASE

There's an endless stream of perpetual
Struggle as I plan my escape from this
Horrific torture chamber, and reach out
From the tears of tyranny an oppression

Into the joyous rays of passive progression
In the still of the night there's much more
Aggressive fight! We all keep longing for
What is right; our bleeding wounds appear

As we shed off the horrendous vagrant disease
Hungry is the heart which gurgles sleeplessly
At night, there's so much hidden fright
Can we be protected by the cosmic light

VAINGLORIOUS PRAISE

I can see the terror leaping out of your eyes
And the sounds of horror screeching from lies
There is no substitute for the utterly destitute
Only a glimmer of hope: in order for you to cope

I've swallowed many words of vainglorious praise
Then I got jolted by your ruby ultra violet rays
Now we can see thru the cloudy, raspy stormy haze
As we shuffle our love past the greyish dark days

VARIED INFECTION

We seldom behave like the naked and the dead!
But we keep copulating in our soft fluffy bed
I'd like to conduct, cognitive investigation
To exploit the untapped subconscious situation

It may incorporate a mediocre non chalant explanation
Harnessing some meticulous scientific experimentation
Thus challenging overlapping emotional interpretation
My mind's eye remains cautiously focused on the harsh

Cracked up earth and vast sand drifting and plains
It's akin to the varied infection of you're soulless
Fledgling nauseating pains, the insidious inflammation
Lies engulfed with bad bacteria and dead tissue stains

Blotching over you're disembodied mind reversing the pliable
Healing process to unwind, hence oscillitating an ultrasonic
Current shock, culminating in an angst ridden orgasmic spam
Are you still trying to resurrect the elusive holy phantasm?

VEHEMENT DELUGE

Your brain screeches like a wornout at tyre
That's so violently ready to crashingly burst
But you still maintain to be the worthy first
Are you suffering from drowsy sleep paralysis

Or afflicted with some strange dialysis?
There's a litany of unhappiness stranded
Upon you're meagre, flimsy pitiful heart
Will you delocalize the vehement deluge?

That's mercilessly tearing you further apart
There's no parking spot available for you to
Stop n'rest then decongest you're jaded head
How can you save someone whose already dead?

VIVID CONTINGENCY

You always say that you wish to try
Out new things n'explore vast worlds
But your too afraid to tip your toes
Into the clear, calm shallow waters

There's a gaping hole on your face
As you look puzzled n' out of place
Are you a hologram, from a strange new race
Hollering aloud in a lonely forgotten space

Our previously grandiose plans have sadly
Filtered down to a mere, gaggling trickle
Unnecessarily staving off the long aspired
Yet elusively desired, renewed renaissance

Is there a vivid contingency package? To ward off
This menacingly fluttering preposterous dalliance
Pointing at the goldenrod of you're ideological dreams
Whilst sipping the grapes of wrath into various themes

WARM N'LOVING FEELING

There can be no presumptions or conclusions
Only straight out facts, without dellusions
There are some things which we cannot understand
Like the feeling when I touch and kiss your hand

Embodying yet groping a warm n'loving feeling
It's akin to seducing a tender happy yearling
Aligning you're shattered heart without stealing
Does love often give and forgive without feeling

WAXING MOONLIGHT

Your pale lusting lips an twilight eyes
Reveal such a delicately sweet surprise
I'm gliding on a snowcapped lover's mountain
So I'll toss another coin, into the fountain

You're unflinching devotion is so subtle n'clean
All my inhibitions fade away so impulsively keen
Our thoughts are blanketed peacefully and serene
The soul ambition is to pursue the lover's dream

Magical feelings in the evening, pleasantly descend
The caressing of waxing moonlight is such a godsend
I will always love you so tenderly warm and forever
Don't worry my dear; because soon we'll be together

WISHFULLY STARE

It's not cyclonic, pounding acid rain that
Has skuttled your mascara down your podgy face
Your shimmering red lips are like sheer dynamite
And imbuing a flumsy hypnotic braggadocio effect

They're cold hearted; as you plainly select
Even though you frolic as the teacher's pet
Be careful not to get all wet. I'd like to throw
My hat high in the air because you lovingly care

Blindly I follow my heart, but your not there
Can I stop to see you or just wishfully stare
The winds of change are shifting us closer together
In a strange sort of labyrinth, we can live forever

WISTFULLY MOPING

I'm wistfully moping at the delicately
Moondrenched skies unreliably spraying
Their contingent of asteroids n'comets n
Space junk vomits, a component of cosmic

Mystery is compelling our seeptical minds
There's a margin of transfer n'withdrawal
And of insufficient consultative measures
Stabbing at my poorly comprehending brain

Is our primitive knowledge scattered in vain?
Do we lack the disbursement of disclosing any
Permanent gain? Can we facilitate an enviable
Advantage, regardless from the cost and pain?

ZEPHYR HUES

The suburban domestic life is very
Disarmingly innocuous, mixed within
A variable of intangible countenance
Inappropriate mediocrity and restless

Trite, that's why I'm now ready to bite
I can't bottle up my irrepressible agility
It's not confined to some in house ability
My barber indecorously adorns my roving

Hippy hirsute and smelly baggy pants
It appears like I've stumbled in from
The paltry chorus rain treading on silvery
Coloured zephyr hues, we can light the flues